Making More Than Lemonade Out of Lemons

Inspiring stories with journaling prompts for thriving through life's most challenging moments.

Betsy Rosam, M.S.

Total Life Solutions, LLC.

Making More Than Lemonade Out of Lemons

All the information in this book is strictly suggestions of the author, based on her own personal experiences. They are meant to inspire not as therapy of any kind. The author and Total Life Solutions, LLC is not liable for any choices, decisions that readers make, or the consequences of any decisions made. All choices are the sole responsibility of those persons making those decisions.

Copyright © 2017 by Betsy Rosam, M.S.(Elizabeth Sine-Rosam)
Total Life Solutions, LLC.

All rights reserved. No part of this book may be reproduced or transmitted in any form or by any means, electronic or mechanical, including photocopying, recording, or by any other information storage and retrieval system now known or later developed ; nor may it be otherwise copied for public or private use without the express written permission of the author, other than 'fair use' as brief quotations embodied in articles and reviews.

For information contact :

Betsy Rosam, M.S.

BetsyRosam.com

ISBN: 978-0-692-94882-8

Introduction:

I first started to write this book prior to one of the biggest challenges that I have yet to have in my life. I had it all ready to publish. I even had my editor make corrections. Something happened that changed my life, so I stopped. I didn't send it off to be published. I didn't market it. I knew that I needed to process what just happened and that I needed to include my growth experiences from it as well.

The challenge was losing my daughter to a drunk driving crash. The loss of a child is one of the most horrifying experiences a parent can go through. As part of this book I will also share how I have experienced the grief and how I continue to work through it daily. I thought it was valuable and important to include it. I've even changed the name of the book, from "What's The Missing Piece?" To "Making More Than Lemonade Out of Lemons", as in this process of grieving, I was directed to make that change.

I have always been a more positive half glass full kind of gal. I've been accused many times of being a "Pollyanna". In spite of this personality trait, I had many limiting beliefs that kept me stuck. One of the most profound one was that I was not good enough. In the work I do, I've found this to be a popular limiting belief. At some point in our lives, we decided this to be true or someone told us and we believed it, and then every situation that vaguely resembled that truth or was in alignment with it, made it stronger. I made the decision to change these limiting beliefs so that I could make more than lemonade out of lemons,

I could make lemon zest, lemon pie and lemon potpourri.

We typically put others first: our kids, family, loved ones, and our business. Much of the time we neglect our self-development, even though studies show that the most successful people take care of themselves first. There is also evidence that happy people are the most productive which creates huge successes in their lives, careers, relationships, parenting, health, and overall wellbeing. Putting off self-development isn't necessarily the best thing for us. We are "the missing piece". We are more important than we give ourselves resources towards. Although this sounds self-centered, it's not, as we can't give from what we don't have. Focusing on our needs and working on ourselves allows us to be better for those people in our lives we love: our family and friends; as well as to be our best in our careers.

I share with you some of my insights to positive change, my experiences, strengths, and hopes. My life's journey thus far has provided me with many lessons. I also share what I have witnessed in regard to the personal development of my many clients. In these short snippets of wisdom, I hope to inspire you for positive personal change and help you to learn how to make more than lemonade out of lemons.

I am an Expert Energy Psychology Spiritual Counselor that recognizes that our success in business is also related to our personal success. I enjoy assisting women business owners move past any blocks, emotional triggers or limiting beliefs that they may have. I understand that many times we put off personal development, but when our thoughts or feelings are not in alignment with our goals in our business, we end up self-sabotaging our success. This is true for successes in our personal life: romantic relationships, family and parenting, as well as friendships.

I have a whole toolbox full of useful skills that I use to guide you in changing any limiting beliefs that may have been programmed into your subconscious mind along the way of your life's journey. As you read these short observations, you'll discover the importance of addressing the subconscious mind and how much it affects our everyday life.

In each chapter I have included questions for you to answer in a journaling format. Space is provided at the end of each chapter for this purpose, as well as creating "tapping scripts". You can utilize them to "tap out the crap; any negative feelings, thoughts, or resistances that have shown up for you during the process. At the end this introduction, I have included a link to my website where you can sign up for a free report on "What Might be Holding You Back", a video on "How To Muscle Test for a Limiting Belief", and a video on "How to Tap Away a Limiting Belief". All of these tools will assist you in utilizing this book in the best way possible.

As a previous Vocational Home Economics Teacher, with a Masters Degree in Mental Health Counseling, and a mother of three grown children, I have vast knowledge and a variety of skills in which to support my clients. My credentials include: Certified EFT Practitioner and Advanced Psych-K© Facilitator. These two Energy Psychology tools in addition to other skills and knowledge make me the perfect consultant to assist you in your TOTAL LIFE TRANSFORMATION! Total Life Solutions, LLC offers just what it says – solutions for your life.

"I am a trauma expert and emotional regenerator. I take women from self sabotage to success guiding them in the release of emotional triggers and limiting beliefs that have kept them stranded on an island of unhappiness. Let me be the one to guide you to your paradise."

BetsyRosam.com

Table of Contents

"Change your thoughts, and you change your world."
Norman Vincent Peale .... page 9

Gratitude 101 .... page 12

Positive Self Esteem is the Key To Happiness ......
.... page 16

Everything's A Miracle .... page 20

"If you can dream it, you can do it." Walt Disney .....
.... page 24

What's the Mess in your Message? .... page 28

Do You Ever *"Flat-line Your Feelings to Avoid the Roller Coaster of Life"?* Betsy Rosam ..... page 30

Life Is Exactly What We Make of It, All the Time! ...
.... page 34

"Failure... is only God pointing us in another direction." BetsyRosam .... page 36

Can Anger Be Useful? *"Anger is really just fear, pain, hurt, or frustration all dressed up in a power suit!"* BetsyRosam .... page 40

Just - What? .... page 44

I Don't Compare My Insides to Someone Else's Outsides page46

You Can't Give What You Don't Have! . . . . page 48

So What's Codependency and How Does It Affect Me? . . . . page 50

Enjoy the Journey! . . . . page 54

It's All About Attitude . . . . page 56

How Are You at Setting Boundaries? . . . . . page 60

What is Real Intimacy? . . . . page 62

Trust Starts with Me . . . . page 64

Living in My Vision, Manifesting My Dreams . page 66

What Are Your Thoughts Around Wealth? . . page 70

Happiness is an inside job . . . . page 72

Another "AHA" Moment! What's Got You Stuck? . . . . page 74

I Am ALL that I say I AM... . . . . page 78

Meditation, is it Really Prayer? . . . . page 80

Living Life With No Regrets . . . . page 84

Forgiveness . . . . page 88

Resource: Meridian Tapping Instructional Sheet . . . . page 92

> *"Change your thoughts,
> and you change your world."*
> Norman Vincent Peale

Many of us are familiar with the Universal Law of Attraction. It says that we attract what we think about, and that our feelings about our thoughts create the energy that draws everything to us. Many of us have worked on changing our thoughts, but we keep attracting the things in our lives that we don't want: relationships, jobs, finances, and uncomfortable situations that don't work for us.

This Universal Law of Attraction works much like the Universal Law of Gravity; it works all of the time, even if we don't believe in it, and not just when we feel up to it. Anytime we hold a thought, a fear, or a worry, we are actually attracting more of what's causing those thoughts or fears in our lives.

How do we change this negative producing thought process? It all starts with our subconscious thoughts, those thoughts of "good enough" that were programmed into our subconscious part of the brain in our early formative years. We could have had wonderful loving kind parents and still have some feelings that were negative, due to a neighborhood bully or a critical teacher. But then some of us had parents that really didn't know how to parent and instilled some limiting beliefs that were harmful to us without knowing it. I am writing this, so as not to place blame, but to have us look inside at what's really stopping us, what's keeping us from being the person we know we can be with the successes we know we are worthy of.

Our subconscious is in charge 95% of the time, through habits. Our conscious beliefs are what we think we believe to be true, but they only operate 5% of the time. Here's how it goes, we think we love ourselves unconditionally, we are acting upon this conscious belief, and yet we meet people that don't like us, or treat us badly. Our conscious belief isn't in alignment with our subconscious belief, as it is the stronger one. Our subconscious gets into alignment with "I'm not good enough". You see, whatever our subconscious mind believes is true, it sets out to keep that truth going, it finds those things like self-sabotage, unhealthy foods, horrible bosses and unfulfilling jobs, etc. The whole time we are thinking with our conscious mind that we are "good enough" and that life is just throwing us these curveballs to duck. Where in this is so far from the truth, our subconscious mind is thinking "I'm not good enough" based on a childhood thought that was programmed so many years ago.

You see, we have an RAS, Reticular Activating System in our brain, its sole purpose is that of a "locator" or "finder". It finds or locates what we are thinking about, and since our subconscious thoughts are in control 95% of the time, guess what? Yep, this is why we are where we are, this is why we don't keep our promises to ourselves. Life isn't throwing us curveballs, we, or our RAS, is finding or locating these situations to be in alignment with the limiting subconscious belief. It really is not our fault, we are only doing what we know how to do. However, there really is a way to change those limiting subconscious beliefs, those ones that don't work to our benefit, the "not good enoughs". This is the work I do with my clients, and the same work I've done for myself.

Journal Question: What are some "limiting beliefs" you might have?

_____

_____

_____

_____

_____

_____

_____

_____

_____

_____

_____

Gratitude 101

"Gratitude, Anger, Resentment & Hatred Cannot Live in Consciousness at the Same Time."

©Betsy Rosam

I learned many years ago the importance of gratitude and how it affects my life. I was first taught to write a gratitude list at a time in my life where I was attempting to save a marriage with an emotionally and verbally abusive husband. I didn't think I had much to be grateful for and it was pointed out to me that I had my health, a roof over my head, and three healthy happy children. As I began to write a daily list, I felt better, and realized that gratitude was a sort of prayer and it kept me focused on the good things in my life. It gave me clarity and helped me to take better care of myself. This led to changes that benefitted both my family and myself. I later divorced and found a wonderful relationship and remarried.

In this process, I learned that gratitude is the armor against all negative thoughts and feelings. How do we stay in the state of grace with gratitude? Here are some tips that I have discovered.

1. Write a gratitude list daily. If you are stumped for a place to begin, using the alphabet would be helpful, or begin with a goal of five things you are grateful for each day.

2. Create a gratitude jar, and each day write the date and something you're grateful for. After my daughter's death, we were cleaning out her

apartment and came across a gratitude jar in which she utilized daily. I found peace in knowing that she too was expressing gratitude in her life, and it explained why she was so happy in her last months. She found that by expressing gratitude, she was attracting more to be grateful for.

3. Take moments during each day to express gratitude to God; a simple "thank you God" (or source, Divine Being, whatever you call your Higher Power) for little things, like a parking spot, or a phone call from a friend. You'd be surprised at how quickly your mood becomes lightened and happy when you express this simply.

4. During challenging times, quickly find something good in the challenge and express gratitude for it. This might be difficult and I've had to really stretch on this one. My husband was diagnosed with a sort of Muscular Dystrophy, and I was devastated at the news, but I knew that if I stayed in fear and sadness, I would attract more of it. I quickly used some Meridian Tapping to release the fears and painful thoughts, and then asked myself what "good" was in this. I found that the type of MD that he had been diagnosed with was inherited and he'd had it since childhood. Knowing that his parents were neglectful in taking him to the doctor and it wasn't diagnosed back then was a blessing, because in the 1960's kids with that kind of diagnosis were institutionalized. I would never have met my sweet heart. Interestingly enough, as time went on and we sought out other neurologists, his diagnosis changed to a lessor neuropathy. I think that our positive attitude attracted the better news and new diagnosis. I believe our thoughts do create our reality.

5. While going through each day, express appreciation to all that have given any type of service to you, thanking them in a more expressive way, not just a verbal thank you. Tell them what they do matters and how much you appreciate and value their service to you. I learned this, as I call it Gratitude in Action, from Duane Cummings, speaker and author of "The Sensational Salesman". When I was at a *Women's Prosperity Network's Unconference* I sat at his VIP lunch table. We spent time masterminding, but what he shared with us was gratitude in action, expressing to the waiter his appreciation for the service he gave, he then asked us all to clear our plates when we were done, showing that appreciation to the server. It made everyone feel good that day. Later, I remembered this when I was at one of the darkest moments of my life, and it lifted me.

When my daughter was on life support after being hit by a drunk driver, our hotel was four blocks from the hospital. Every morning they served a hot breakfast for their guests as part of the hotel fee. It included eggs, grits, fresh fruit and a variety of breads and juices. The second morning of our stay, I remembered what Duane had taught us, gratitude in action, and I approached the young woman that was serving breakfast that morning. I told her how appreciative I was of her getting up early and creating such a wonderfully nutritious breakfast for us. I shared with her that many of us residing there at the hotel were spending most of our days at the hospital and that this might be the only decent meal we would get that day. My daughter's crash had been all over the news and I shared that with her as well, and that she was on life support. She hugged me and shared that her four year old son had cancer and we shared a quiet prayer for our children. We made each other's day, all from a simple act of gratitude and kindness.

6. End each day with a prayer of gratitude. I can always find something to be grateful about, and when I do this at the end of the day, I sleep well.

<u>Journal Question:</u> What ways do you express gratitude?

_____

_____

_____

_____

_____

_____

_____

_____

_____

Positive Self Esteem is the Key To Happiness
"Self Love is the steering wheel on our life's journey."
Betsy Rosam

I was on a conference call this morning and the topic was about loving oneself. Many of us did not have this thought. As a little girl I was taught that self-love was self centered and conceited, and no one likes people that are conceited. I took that in and allowed it to control my life in many unhealthy ways. Many of us heard as children that we needed to do better to be better, and it left many of us with feelings of "not good enough".

I was told that I was five pounds at birth and that I had no hair and my ears stuck out. My mother explained this to me many times in a very apologetic way, and that she had taped my ears back, trying to force them to stay back, but that didn't work. I was doomed to forever not wear my hair behind my ears. I was also told that I was so small that they carried me around on a pillow out of fear of dropping me and that I needed expensive formula. My spitting up all the time was a problem as well.

My full name is Elizabeth Ann, my father named me after his two sisters. My mother wanted to name me something else, but she did not come out of anesthesia early enough, and my dad had beat her to it and filled out the birth certificate before my mother was alert. My mother was a stubborn woman, and dealt with it in another way, one which began a journey of "not good enough's" for me. She decided, I was told later, to call me Sissy, because I was told my brother couldn't say sister. So I reasoned to myself that if he could have pronounced sister, that would have been my name until I was ten. I decided that I wasn't even good enough for my own name. As you can imagine I attracted all kinds of negative situations in my life with that belief and struggled for many years to finally "love myself" from the inside out.

I had done a lot of personal development through various workshops, classes and support groups. I thought I had cleared that belief from my being. However, when I was working with a PSYCH-K© practitioner, she used kinesiology to show me that my subconscious still believed that "I wasn't good enough". We did a brain balance (part of PSYCH-K©) on this belief and replaced it with "I love myself unconditionally". It took less than five minutes, and it has changed my life forever.

Since then, people remark about how happy and radiant I am. My relationships are better today, because I no longer have that belief. I am able to work through issues quickly and confidently. I speak openly with a sense of reverence and wisdom about what I have learned, and I have a connection with the God of my understanding that I have never had before. It's amazing what "falling in love" with myself has done for me.

When working with my clients, that is the very first "limiting belief" that we clear. I can't tell you how many people also have this belief of "not good enough" from whatever childhood memory they took into their subconscious. Just changing that one belief on the subconscious level changes everything. Have you "fallen in love" with yourself?

Journal Question: What are the qualities that you love about yourself?

Everything's A Miracle

"There are only two ways to live your life. One is as though nothing is a miracle. The other is as though everything is a miracle." anonymous

When I live as though everything is a miracle, I am appreciative and grateful. That positive energy is like a shield against negative thoughts that lead to feelings I don't like. Because I am in gratitude, I deflect those thoughts as well as those feelings.

Have you ever noticed a person that seems to have the worse situations occurring to them, like all the time? It's not just a cycle, but over and over again they seem to attract it, and you find them talking about their problems repeatedly? Conversely, there are people that appear to have the Midas touch, everything they do turns to gold, they are filled with gratitude, and ridiculously happy. I think those are the people that believe everything's a miracle, and rejoice in life, all of it.

For a long time I had a positive attitude and seemed to look for the good in everything; I was even accused of being "Pollyanna", and told to stop playing the "glad game". I gave in and started to focus on my problems, not looking for solutions or silver linings. Guess what? I got more problems, bigger problems! Some of them looked as if they came right out of a soap opera! I looked at it all in disbelief, wondering if this is what I really wanted in my life.

A shift came from watching the movie "The Secret", and I knew there was more to this "Law of Attraction" than just wanting things. I did a lot of studying and found that this Law of Attraction was at work all the time, just like the Law of Gravity. I didn't have to do anything! I attracted what I was, and how I felt!

So my real challenge was to change my thoughts, I was on my way! I started using affirmations to change my thoughts, and they worked for awhile. But then I realized that I needed to believe the affirmations, and that my feelings about my situations were so much more important in this process. I had no idea that my subconscious mind was in charge of my daily habits.

Once I learned how to change my subconscious limiting beliefs, I made real permanent changes in me that were in alignment with everything I wanted in my life! I have attracted a wonderful loving relationship, loving accepting friends, and a welcoming home that just happened to be one that I had picked out four years before buying it. These are only a few of the miracles that have shown up in my life. Today I know that everything is Holy, everything is a miracle, and I treat it as such.

<u>**Journal Question:**</u> **What are the miracles in your life?**

_____

_____

_____

_____

"If you can dream it, you can do it." Walt Disney

Our imagination is very powerful; whatever we imagine, we can create. Where our focus lies, is where our intentions are, and intentions can be powerful. Just think about where Walt Disney came from and all that he created, all that has evolved from his dreams. Where are your thoughts? Where is your focus? Think about what's going on in your life and what makes you happy\. Are they in alignment? If you are so far away from where you want to be, then you most likely need to redirect your focus and change your mind. Many times we know what we don't want, and haven't taken the time to really decide what we want. We often go through life in "default", not actually deciding on what we want, accepting only what life throws at us. This many times results in a roller coaster ride through life that can make us dizzy emotionally.

Using your imagination to see where you want to be and what you want your life to look like creates an intention. Once you do this, and you keep your focus on that, opportunities, ideas and people start showing up to assist you. Your responsibility then is to take action. You must believe enough in what you want, that it is possible for it to happen, to take the right action. I heard somewhere the phrase "Imagination without action is just entertainment." There is so much truth to this.

So many times we have limiting beliefs in our subconscious that stops us somewhere in the middle of this process. Maybe at the beginning, when we are imagining our dream, we hear a voice that might say "no, not you". Or when an idea, opportunity, or person shows up, you deny that they are there for you. Your "not good enough's" may kick in. These self-sabotaging thoughts were programmed in your subconscious at a young age and they are the real culprits to your success.

When people say "all you have to do is change your mind", it sounds easy, but how do you really do it? You can consciously change your mind, but if your subconscious doesn't change, you keep doing the same thing over and over again, expecting different results, the definition of insanity. How do I know about this? Well, I've been through it, and I've used some wonderful energy psychology tools to "Change My Beliefs Into Knowing". I've gotten rid of those "thought gremlins" that created havoc in my life.

Journal Questions: What is it that you want? What are some of the thought gremlins that keep you stuck?

_____

_____

_____

_____

_____

What's the Mess in your Message?

I awoke with some thoughts that I needed to not only write down, but also share. I've gone through many traumas in my life, more than most, and I don't share this for sympathy, as I've also managed to work through them all and live very happily. In fact, most people have no idea to the extent of what I've experienced. Some day I will write another book about them all, but it's overwhelming and it needs to include not only the grief, but also the triumph over each situation.

For quite awhile, I've been struggling with my message of how do I express what I do in my business. I've heard very loudly make your "mess" your "message", and quite honestly I've asked myself, "which one", as there have been so many. Then tonight, or rather this morning, early morning it came to me "all of them"; you have experienced these things so that you can help others. This all made so much sense to me; it gave purpose to all of those events.

Statistics tell us that many of us have experienced abuse, whether it is physical, emotional, mental or sexual. This is trauma that I have experienced, and have worked through using some magnificent tools. I am able to speak about these situations without feeling the emotional pain that they used to carry with them, and because of this I am able to use what happened to me to help others through their pain. Everything we experience and what we thought about those experiences gets set in our subconscious. Some of those thoughts are beneficial to us, others, those resulting from trauma are often not beneficial. They keep us stuck. They create dis-ease.

When we understand that our subconscious thoughts control our lives through habit 95% of the time, if we have limiting core beliefs, like "I am unworthy" or "I am unlovable", they control our outcomes. Everything we do is congruent and in alignment to those beliefs, as they are our truths. Isn't it time to identify your mess and include it in your message, in a way that no longer "triggers" you?

Journal Questions: What traumatic situations have you survived? What still triggers you? How can you use your "mess in your message"?

_____

_____

_____

_____

_____

_____

_____

_____

_____

_____

Do You Ever "Flat-Line Your Feelings to Avoid the Roller Coaster of Life"? Betsy Rosam

I had a conversation recently that got me thinking about feelings and their purpose in our lives. Just this year there was a wonderful kids's movie called "Inside Out" that was all about this topic and if you saw it, you most likely understood the importance of all of our feelings. We live in a world of duality, one of opposites, ups and downs, bigs and littles, etc.

I remember a particularly terrible time in my life when I didn't feel my feelings, I was pretty much numb; I'd call it a flat-line for feelings, and it felt safe. I had been on the rollercoaster, not a little one, but one of the most extreme in my life, and when I think about that time, I probably didn't handle it the best. I didn't take care of me; I lost me in the mess. I didn't want to feel those extreme feelings, so I chose to feel numb. For quite some time I walked around with a fake smile on my face, not feeling anything. Later, I discovered this wasn't healthy either; I was pushing the feelings down, burying them, only to surface later, in a very unhealthy way.

At one point, while I was doing some internal work, I decided that I wanted to feel the good feelings again; love, compassion, joy. I surrounded myself with people, places, and things that I thought made me happy. I then figured out that the joy was inside and that it was up to me to share it with others. In this process, some things began to happen, because, well, that's life. Those things that were hard to deal with, they hurt, and I felt pain. I was afraid that I'd be on that roller coaster again, but instead of pulling back, I pushed through. I realized that in order to feel, I had to feel everything, and everything was messy, but authentic and real, and those connections were the best, and didn't I deserve the best?

Because of duality, we can't really understand joy, without knowing the opposite, fear. Darkness is the absence of light; roses have thorns. Flat line living was tasteless, gray, and dull.

Even though I do choose to live on the roller coaster of life, I don't allow it to be extreme. I choose what to do with my feelings, I have the tools to diffuse them, so that I don't feel sick, and when the difficult ones show up, it's not an extreme roller coaster. Today I can cry with a friend when I need to, and enjoy love and laughter as well. I embrace all of my feelings, and allow them to surface, face them, work through the tough ones, and release them. Life is so much more bountiful and abundant because I have chosen to face it. Flat lining my feelings has lost it's appeal.

<u>**Journal Questions:**</u> **What are some feelings that you want to deny? How has that worked for you? What are some things you'd like to change?**

_____

_____

_____

_____

Life Is Exactly What We Make of It, All the Time!

I have to remember this when I feel in what I call a "funk", that this place I'm in, is exactly where I choose to be at this moment. I don't want to be hard on myself, because that's never been helpful either, but I do want to look at why I've chosen to be in this particular "funk" at this moment in time.

Several things come to my mind. First, I might be thinking about the past, which usually means I am wishing I had done something or many things differently, and had different outcomes. My intelligence knows that it's impossible to change the past, and yet, I visit this place, which might very well have led me into this "funk" at this time. Another reason I am here in this miserable place, where I am procrastinating, blaming, shaming, and feeling like crap in general, is because I might be looking to the future with fear, and when I do that, I am hopeless.

WOW! I am in charge! My thinking is creating this funk, and all of the blaming, shaming, and feeling stuck is leading me to the outcomes, or lack of outcomes in my life.

With this I know that being right here, right now, is powerful; because right here and right now, there is no blame, shame, procrastination, stuck. Right here and right now, all is good; in fact, better than good. If I stay right here, and right now, not one minute before or after, I am creating this wonderful tapestry in my life. If my right here, right now, has challenges in it, I slip into finding gratitude in it, and it's all good. For me, I am the "silver lining queen", and I make the most of every situation, and guess what? My life is exactly what I make of it, all the time - Pretty darn great!

Journal Questions: How does staying in the "Now" help you? What are some thoughts that keep you in yesterday and fearful of tomorrow? How do you deal with a "funk"?

_____

_____

_____

_____

_____

_____

_____

_____

_____

_____

_____

"Failure... is only God pointing us in another direction." Betsy Rosam

Without failure, there is no success.

I find it amazing how many people allow the fear of failure to stop them in their tracks. If we truly look at the history of any successful person or inventor, we find that they failed repeatedly, and yet continued until they were successful. They knew that failure was like a compass, pointing them down the path that they needed to go down, tweaking the experiment, or changing their direction. They knew that failure is part of any success.

When we are afraid of failing, and we don't see it as a positive thing, we don't move, we don't try, we don't attempt that which our soul longs for. We actually become the failure that we are so fearful of, we fail to try, we fail to go forward in the direction that we are lead.

Overly concerned parents may have taught this fear of failure to us. They wanted to protect us from failure, or they insisted on perfection, this caused us to be focused on our outcome and not the journey.

In the process, we find our way towards success, and failures are part of that process. They are the indicators that, if we pay attention to and adjust from, we move closer to our goals. When we don't see the failures as part of the journey and we take them in as shame, we lose. We aren't a failure; it's that our process is just in need of some redirection.

I remember as a child, I had received straight A's up until the 4th grade. I had a teacher that gave us an assignment to read 6 books and write 6 book reports. Well, I had misunderstood her and thought she said 5, so I read the 5 books and wrote up the same number of book reports. I loved to read and this was an enjoyable assignment for me and when I turned them in, I was proud of my work. To my devastation, she gave me an "F", not only on the assignment, but on my report card. I took that shame in, and allowed that failure to dictate many of my academic decisions and behaviors for years. It took a long time for me to finally let go of the shame from that particular failure. I certainly wish I had understood as a child that it was only a misunderstanding that I could correct by changing my mind about it, and letting go of the shame that took me in so many painful directions.

Thankfully, I was able to make those changes that allow me to make mistakes today, knowing that those errors are simply tools to guide me to the right and perfect places in my life. I am grateful. I am blessed.

Journal Questions: **What fears about success and failures do you have? What's a message from a situation that has held you back?**

_____

_____

_____

_____

Can Anger Be Useful?
"Anger is really just fear, pain, hurt, or frustration all dressed up in a power suit!"
Betsy Rosam

So many times we hear that anger is harmful to us, and it does create stress in our lives, but only if we don't check in on it. You see, anger does have a purpose in our lives. It's a sort of compass that tells us something's not right. Anger worn over a long period of time is what really hurts us. Anger has the illusion of power, until we lose our temper, then we are actually shown as being weak.

If we really look into our anger, it's usually a cover up for another feeling, because we fall into the trap of thinking that anger sure feels better and more powerful than fear, hurt or pain. And frustration is also known as a weak, helpless, powerless feeling. In order to release the anger, we do need to identify what it really is about. I know people that wear their anger like a badge of courage, a wall to keep others out. When we do this, we are not being our authentic selves; we were meant to be happy, gracious, healthy people. If you find yourself even the slightest irritable at most everything; look into what's really going on. Take this time for yourself, you deserve it.

I am angry, but not at any one person or thing. I think the anger is about the unfairness of it all. She was my beautiful 34-year old daughter, soon to be celebrating her 35th birthday and telling me how she was the happiest she'd ever been in her whole life. She and her boyfriend had planned a Christmas cruise with his parents and they were talking about a future together; these two elementary school music teachers that had met in college, and reconnected six months ago.

They say that anger is part of the grieving process, not sure who "they" are, until yesterday, I didn't think so. You see, a drunk driver killed her. It is thought to be his 3rd DUI, and you'd think that I would be angry at him for making this choice. But, having spent more than 25 years in a support group for friends and family members of alcoholics, I know better. I have friends and family members that have been in jail or should have been in jail for DUI's. I am familiar with the pain of a parent with a child in jail. No, his family lost their child that day. I am not angry with him, more than likely I am angry at the disease of alcoholism and addiction that is stealing our children from us. I am grateful that I am not his parent; my pain is horrific, and theirs is too, although much different.

Now, what did I do with my anger? I let it out in excruciating, embarrassing, and painful cries. I spent a good hour or so with this process. I allowed all of the feelings to wash over me as I released them into the universe, knowing that the God of my understanding, along with my angels are always with me, holding me in love. The next day I woke up late, allowing myself the time to sleep and heal, and decided to do my meditation outside, since it was so beautiful. I took my angel cards out and picked three of them. They happened to be: Surrender and Release, Freedom, and Emerging; all very important to me at that time. Meditation is listening to God; I am listening with an open heart and releasing the anger that covers my pain and hurt. Losing a child is one of the most difficult challenges a parent can face and each day I release a little more of the hurt and pain, and move into honoring her memory.

Journal Questions: What things get you angry? What might really be behind the anger?

Just ~ What?

Lately I've been hearing people using the word "just" as a descriptive of them or of something. An example might be, "I am just doing xyz". Just used in that context is limiting. I don't think people realize that when we use that word in that frame of reference, that we are coming from a place of limitation and lack.

I remember when I first met my husband. I was with a group of about 12 friends for dinner and he was sitting at the other end of the table. He later told me that he asked the woman sitting next to him who I was; her reply was "oh, that's just Betsy". We didn't see each other for another year when we met again through friends. I hadn't remembered him, but he remembered me as "just Betsy". When he told me this story, I found myself questioning the word "just". The woman who introduced me didn't have my best interest at heart, or she wouldn't have used that word to describe me. If you really know me, I am anything other than "just Betsy". After that experience, I started noticing how often people use the word "just" in that limiting way.

As a prayer chaplain, I even hear it in prayers, just …. just… just… I was blown away that we would even use this limiting language in our conversations with God the omnipowerful and omnipresent. I am aware of the voice and language I use today, as I believe there is power in our words. Now I use the word just, as it was intended, a shortened form of justice, not as a way to place limitations on anything.

Journal Questions: Think about what you want in life, what you want more of, is it "just" anything? Is "just" a habit that you utilize? When do you find yourself using the word "just"?

_____
_____
_____
_____
_____
_____
_____
_____
_____
_____
_____
_____
_____

I Don't Compare My Insides to Someone Else's Outsides

I don't compare my insides to someone else's outsides. Because… Well first of all, we really don't know what's going on for someone else; we only see what they allow us to see. They may be struggling with situations and challenges that we would never want to have in our lives. And secondly, we need to embrace who we are. Our unique situations are meant for us, we have chosen them all for the lessons we need to learn.

If we are not happy with what's going on in our lives, we should be looking inward, not outward. All of our answers are within. Some questions I usually ask myself are: for what purpose am I going through this, what's the lesson for me, or even what in me or my attitude has attracted this? These questions usually lead me to answers that help me to deal with the situation I am going through. I've learned that if I don't change me in the situation, that the same scenario usually comes back, only with different people, places, or things involved.

What I've learned is that I need to do my work and not wish it away, dreaming that I could have someone else's life. Their life really might be more challenging than mine, and theirs aren't the lessons I need to learn to move to who I am truly meant to be.

Journal Questions: What comparisons do you make? How do they help/hinder you?

You Can't Give What You Don't Have!

How many times have you been given a gift or a favor and discounted it or not even accepted it, saying something like "oh no, you shouldn't have"? When we do this, we think somehow it shows that we are generous, but does it really? It may appear to be humbling, but it actually selfishly removes the joy of giving in the situation. The loving energetic vibration behind the action of giving and receiving is diminished. This is something I have become aware of in my life recently, an awakening to the importance of being fully present in the giving and receiving course.

When we talk about the giving and receiving circle, we have to also look at an imbalance we may have created in a relationship by constantly giving, and not expecting anything in return. This cycle requires balance. We cannot give from an empty well and certainly cannot give what we don't have.

When one side of a relationship does the giving and the other the receiving, there is a balance between the two, but not within each individual. We have by our "only giving" taught the other person to be "only the receiver". By this action, we have robbed them of the joy of giving, and us of the joy of receiving. It really has to be a two-way street.

I think that this is an important conversation, especially for women and moms, who give tirelessly to their families. I wonder if they have noticed the imbalance they may have created in their families by doing and giving everything for everyone in their families. Looking back at my parenting behaviors, I know I was guilty of this, and wonder how it has affected my children and their ability to be "giving" adults in a relationship. I'm sure the imbalance of giving and receiving that I modeled, taught them to be one or the other, the giver or the receiver, as they didn't experience a balance of this cycle. This is one of my regrets as a parent.

Since we really only have now, and anything in the past cannot be relived, we can utilize it as a lesson to learn from. I'm hoping these thoughts inspire you to look at what you are teaching the people in your life.

Journal Questions: Are you being the example of a receiver and a giver, are you in balance? What areas do you need to change?

_____

_____

_____

_____

_____

_____

_____

So What's Codependency and How Does It Affect Me?

You've probably heard the term "codependency" before and maybe wondered, or not, if it relates to you. Anyone that has done personal development work has most likely heard of it before. But how do we know if we are codependent and if we are, how do we change it? After all, it's a personality trait that was most likely learned when we were younger.

The idea of codependence comes directly out of Alcoholics Anonymous, "part of a dawning realization that the problem was not solely the addict, but also the family and friends who constitute a network for the alcoholic." The family or friends enable the alcoholic by catering to their every whim, putting their needs and wants above their own. If you were raised in a family where alcoholism or addiction was present, you most likely learned codependent behaviors.

Codependency depicts behaviors, thoughts, and feelings that go beyond normal kinds of self-sacrifice or care taking. Codependent people often take on the role of mother hen; they consistently put others' needs before their own and in turn don't take the time to take care of themselves. This establishes an impression that they are "needed"; they cannot take the thought of being alone with no one needing them. Codependent people search for acceptance. Only those caring behaviors that are excessive to an unhealthy degree are considered to be codependent. Codependency breeds "victims"; if you are constantly putting others' needs before your own, you can't help but feel taken advantage of and feeling like a martyr.

When codependency patterns are not resolved, it can lead to more serious problems like alcoholism, drug addiction, eating disorders, sex addiction, and other self-defeating or self-destructive behaviors. Codependent people are also more likely to:

*attract further abuse from aggressive individuals
*more likely to stay in stressful jobs or relationships
*less likely to seek medical attention when needed
*less likely to get promotions
*tend to earn less money than those without codependency patterns

If you find that you are struggling with codependency behaviors, there is a belief system that sustains them. Those beliefs were set up in our subconscious minds during childhood and will continue to cause problems unless we change them.

Journal Questions: Do you have any co-dependency behaviors? What are they? Who do you react co-dependently with?

_____

_____

_____

_____

Enjoy the Journey!

Have you ever been on a trip and taken a wrong turn or your GPS sent you in the wrong direction and as your traveling on the road, you realize that this detour is quite beautiful and fascinating? If you had never taken the wrong turn, or went the wrong way, you would have missed the beauty that was there.

Have you ever taken a path in your life that at first didn't seem right? Then as time progressed, you realized it was perfect for you.

We are all on a journey and what we make of every moment is what we get. When things have appearances of "wrong" or "right" and we judge them to be so, we might be missing out on the real purpose of those moments. If we look beyond and just enjoy the journey, life becomes very precious and we can really "see" the beauty that surrounds us in all things. So I say, "Enjoy the journey!"

Journal Questions: What wrong turns have you made that have turned out to be blessings?

_____

_____

_____

_____

It's All About Attitude

While I was at my Writer's Wings monthly meet up group, we were given a writing assignment to write about our feelings if we were on our way somewhere on the highway and got stuck for 12 hours by a traffic pile up. I wrote this about myself and it shows how my perspective in life has changed. I know for sure today that my attitude has everything to do with how my life goes.

"As she heard the sirens, she felt gratitude, knowing that she was far away from the accident and was safe. In her prayers of gratitude, she asked that those involved be taken care of, and that their families would be comforted in their healing processes. She released a huge sigh of relief and looked at her husband who was sitting next to her, feeling grateful that it was him and not her ex that she would be trapped in this space for the next 12 hours.

It would have been so different. If she had been in a car with her first husband, she would have been miserable. He would have hijacked her emotions to the place of not good enoughs, and she would have gone there with him, not realizing it, until it was too late to escape. He had a way of bringing her to the past and throwing her mistakes in her face, or transporting her to the future where he knew that fear would envelop and paralyze her.

Thankfully, she had made enough changes in her life where she chose to be with a man that loved her unconditionally and never took her to that place of not good enoughs. Their lives, even in the calamities, were filled with humor, love and joy! She knew that this experience today would mimic those emotions as well. She was thankful that they had packed a lunch for their short trip to Melbourne and that they had left the lawn chairs in the trunk of the car from their last beach day.

As Betsy turned to Ray to give him a big hug she knew that in this moment they were going to turn lemons into lemonade again, like so many other times they had done so. Their choices were simple, should they put the convertible hood down and eat lunch? Or should they pull out the lawn chairs and get to know their highway neighbors? As she thought of these choices, she was reminded of gratitude again, and what choices laid ahead for those people in the traffic pileup. She said a silent prayer again for them, and asked their angels to surround them in love.

Now off to meet and socialize with the others who were inconvenienced by this tragic event. Who knows the interesting people we'll meet, she thought as they opened the trunk of the car and she smiled to herself."

After writing this short story, I realized how much I am living in an attitude of gratitude and the positive effects it has on my life.

Journal Questions: What attitudes do you have that you might want to change?

How Are You at Setting Boundaries?

Do you ever feel taken advantage of? Are you attracting people in your life that only take from you? Do you have a hard time saying "No"? Do you feel there is little or no respect in your relationships?

It's important to set boundaries, its a way of taking care of ourselves. We have a responsibility to teach others how to treat us through setting healthy boundaries.

What's the difference between a boundary and a manipulation? When we set a boundary, we let go of the outcome. We explain our feelings and what's not acceptable to us. For example, you might say I feel hurt when you flirt with my best friend, and I would like it to stop. Then you let go of it. If it continues, then you have a choice to make, as this boundary is realistic and respectful. You may need to express that it feels disrespectful and that respect is a quality that you require in a relationship. If it continues, then you would most likely end the relationship, as the boundary wasn't respected or honored.

Boundaries need to be realistic and reasonable. If you have lots of boundaries, you might want to consider that you are trying to control too much of the relationship, and question why that is. Maybe the relationship isn't healthy and you feel the need to control it, or maybe you lack trust because of your own history.

If you have no boundaries, then you have no self-respect and low self-esteem. Both scenarios require some work in order to be able to have healthy realistic boundaries in a relationship. If you find that you are struggling with setting boundaries or honoring others' boundaries, there is most likely a block, a limiting belief in your subconscious that is continually sabotaging intimacy in your relationships. Those types of beliefs were set up in our subconscious mind when we were young and will continue to cause us problems unless we change them.

Journal Questions: How are you at setting healthy boundaries? What boundaries do you think would be good for you to set?

What is Real Intimacy?

So many times when we hear the word intimacy, we immediately think of sex. But true intimacy begins with ourselves and our ability to connect with another human being. Generally, intimacy is defined as the feeling of being in a close personal relationship, a feeling of belonging. It's close connection is a result of bonding that happens when we acknowledge and experience each other. Genuine intimacy requires dialogue, transparency, vulnerability, reciprocity.

To keep intimacy in a relationship, there needs to be a well developed emotional and interpersonal awareness. In real intimacy, both parties keep their separate identities and yet have a togetherness that appears to be unbreakable.

Intimate behavior joins family members and close friends as well as those in love from a place of self-awareness and self-distinction. It grows through mutual self-disclosure and honesty. Poor skills in developing intimacy can lead to:

*getting too close too soon
*struggling with boundaries (both setting healthy ones and honoring other's boundaries)
*not knowing how to be a good friend
*refusing self-disclosure
*dismissing friendships that are healthy

It's been said I can't give what I don't have, and if you find you are struggling with intimacy, there is most likely a block, a limiting belief in your subconscious that is continually sabotaging intimacy in your relationships. Those beliefs were set up in our subconscious minds when we were young and will continue to cause us intimacy problems unless we change them.

Journal Questions: **What intimacy issues do you struggle with? How does it affect your life and relationships?**

_____

_____

_____

_____

_____

_____

_____

_____

_____

_____

_____

Trust Starts with Me

In order to trust others, we need to first trust ourselves. If you are constantly unsure of yourself, questioning your decisions, then you have some trust issues within yourself. Maybe you trusted someone that was untrustworthy and you feel like you failed in listening to your own gut instincts. When this happens the lesson isn't about not trusting yourself again, but to listen to your intuition and trust it wholeheartedly, as not everyone deserves our trust.

Usually when we have failed ourselves in the area of trust, it's not because our intuition wasn't correct, it's usually because we didn't believe or trust it. Many times we look to others to help us make our decisions; they aren't walking in our shoes and living from our perspective, but our limiting beliefs tell us that we aren't capable of making "those" decisions, whatever they may be. We may trust others more than ourselves, and usually that's where we get into trouble, especially if the others we trust are not trustworthy.

These beliefs were set up in our subconscious minds when we were young and will continue to cause us to second-guess our decisions and trusting our selves and others, until we change them.

<u>Journal Questions:</u> How does trusting/not trusting yourself show up in your relationships? Do you lack trust in others?
_____

Living in My Vision, Manifesting My Dreams

This week has been filled with some wonderful lessons, one of which was how to decide if a path that showed up in my life was one that would take me closer towards my dreams or sidetrack me from them. I have had a tendency to be distracted from what is mine to do.

My husband and I have been taking Mary Morrisey's Prosperity Plus 10-week workshop and we had our final class on Thursday evening. The Wednesday before, I got a phone call about a possible job opportunity. It would have been full-time and given me hours I could use to get my Florida Therapist's license. The job itself would have been very fulfilling and I was told that the employer and employees were terrific and it was a wonderful place to work.

While emailing my resume to the director, I had some feelings of uncertainty and found myself wondering if I was offered the job, whether I would take it or not. I was wondering if it was an opportunity or a diversion from my dream. I found myself saying a prayer that I wouldn't get called for an interview, and then I wouldn't have to decide, I let go and let God.

The next evening in our final class, Mary Morrisey discussed the importance of living from our vision, living into it, meaning that we imagined how it felt to live in our dream. So I went home that evening and imagined living in that job and what it felt like, and then living in my vision and what that felt like. My decision to continue onward building momentum in my business became very clear to me. I got a call the next day from my friend and she explained that the job I sent my resume in was filled, little did she know how relieved I felt. She then explained about another part-time position that I might be interested in. As she began to describe it, I interrupted her and explained how that job, even though it was part-time, did not fit into my vision and dreams for my future. I thanked her for thinking of me, sharing my appreciation for her consideration and ended the conversation. WOW! How amazing it is coming from a place of joy and imagination, rather than fear and lack.

For those of you that don't know, last year my husband was diagnosed with Muscular Dystrophy and he had been driving three or more hours a day to his stress filled job. This April was his last day of work, as he decided to fulfill his lifetime dream of becoming a Realtor. Knowing that at this time, he isn't bringing in an income, I could have become immobilized with fear and had the knee jerk reaction to take a job that paid very little and was not in alignment with my vision and dreams.

Interestingly, I had a workshop planned for that Saturday, and by Thursday I only had four people signed up. At my weekly women's intention circle, I had "intended" to have eight in this small intimate workshop. Thursday evening during our Prosperity Plus class, my husband and I discussed what we would tithe this week. We had agreed to tithe 10% of our income at the beginning of the class, but his question was "what's 10% of nothing?". We decided as a couple that in regards to our tithing we would act "as if", so we wrote the check for the 10% of what I would make if I had the eight clients I had intended in my workshop on Saturday.

All of this was happening at the same time as I was "deciding" whether to take the "dangling carrot" in the form of a job or not. Remember I stated that on Thursday evening, I only had four people signed up for my class that Saturday? The next day, the final four people registered! It's as if the universe responded to my intentions because I acted "as if". Those intentions had the energy of money in the form of tithing behind them.

The workshop was amazing and it's success was an affirmation of my decision to move forward with my business, living from my vision, and letting go of the fear and lack that may have swayed me to decide to take a job that wasn't mine to do. I'm hoping that my experience will lead you in discerning what's in your best interest. Remember to live in the vision and dream!

<u>**Journal Questions:**</u> **What visions and dreams are you manifesting or have manifested? How does remembering them help you now?**

_____

_____

_____

_____

_____

What Are Your Thoughts Around Wealth?

I am reading "Secrets of the Millionaire Mind" and doing some PSYCH-K© balances on some of the beliefs about wealth that I had. It's an awesome book about our beliefs about money, wealth, abundance and prosperity. Interestingly, the past three clients I had, we did balances on prosperity mindset. So many of us "baby boomers" had parents that survived "the great depression" and many of their money beliefs were passed onto us.

If some of the things you heard about money were: "Money doesn't grow on trees", "You have to work hard to get ahead", "We can't afford it", "Rich is what other people are, not us", and "Rich people are snobs"; you most likely have some limiting beliefs that have prevented you from being financially prosperous. Think of some of the negative sayings around money that you've heard.

In order to create wealth in your life, you have to change those old beliefs that aren't working for you anymore. If you thought rich people were greedy and you are a nice person, you won't attract rich, and if you do, you won't keep it.

How many of us know of or have heard of people that have been "poor" and then won the lottery or came into a huge sum of money, only to be "poor" again in a year or two? It's about our beliefs deep down in our subconscious. Suze Orman says money problems are never about the money. Isn't it time you change your mind about money?

Journal Questions: What are some limiting beliefs around money that you heard as a child? How do you think these have played out in your life?

_____
_____
_____
_____
_____
_____
_____
_____
_____
_____
_____
_____
_____
_____

Happiness is Inside Job

How can we create our own happiness, joy and bliss? If we are battling with those voices that say we're not good enough, or we can't do this or that, or someone else does it better, then it's difficult to find joy in our lives. Those little, I call them "pop up ads" in our mind, need to be squelched, in order for us to move forward and have our best life.

These little negative thoughts create more negativity in our lives - we create what we are thinking... So how do we get rid of them and have positive "pop up ads", like "you can do it", "you're the greatest", and "oh yeah go for it!" There are several things you can do to create happiness in your life and to let go of those limiting beliefs that can enslave us. Meditation first and foremost has helped me. At first, I had to utilize guided meditations, then later I could go "into the silence" and not have the "monkey mind chatter" go on, and be in the silence. Other things have helped me to tap into the happiness inside of me.

Those who have one or more close friendships are happier. Cooperatively being engaged in activities and sharing our personal feelings is what makes a difference, expressing genuine interest and voicing what's in our hearts. Expressing kindness consistently leads to being happier and less depressed. Any time we are helpful, it boosts our feelings. Also a lower incidence of depression has been related to movement and eating well.

Setting realistic goals and achieving them creates joy. We are in our "flow". Be active in your life, do what you enjoy doing. Find what you intrinsically value; don't depend on "outside" things to provide your happiness. We know what "floats our boat" and gives us joy.

There is a link between spiritual and religious practice and happiness. Determine what is spiritually important to you and develop a deeper kind of happiness. Recognize and use your strengths. The happiest people are those that have identified their unique strengths and virtues and use them for a purpose that is greater than for their own personal goals. Express gratitude in all things, in all ways as grateful people have been shown to have more positive emotions, a larger sense of belonging, and lower incidence of depression and stress.

Journal Questions: What ways are you going to tap into the joy and happiness that resides within you?

_____

_____

_____

_____

_____

_____

Another "AHA" Moment! What's Got You Stuck?

I know the importance of our subconscious thoughts in regards to what's going on in our lives. After all, I work with my clients helping them to change any limiting subconscious beliefs, therefore bettering their lives.

For the past few years I have struggled with my weight, and know that part of the weight gain was due to thyroid tumors, and the removal of my thyroid. I had been a thin person for the first half of my life. Even after having three children, I could still wear a bikini and turn heads. So this person I had become was uncomfortable and difficult to accept. During some insight about my situation, I came to understand that I am responsible for about 50% of the weight gain and the rest is due to the thyroid issue. I am taking responsibility for my part. I also know that there is a limiting belief that is keeping me stuck; I just wasn't sure what that was.

After some prayer, meditation, and reflection, a thought came to me. I shared it with my husband, and in that moment I realized what the limiting belief was that was holding me back from a healthy vibrant lifestyle. I knew what work I had to do.

Later that day, I was putting away some magazines from my Vision Board Workshop, and came across a significant photo and article from the June 2012 Issue of Glamour. It was titled "The Secret Way People Are Judging You". The photo was of two women, one was of large stature and the other was of a slim one. There were words written on each photo based on their stereotype labels judged by most. On the slim woman was written vain, bitchy, superficial, ambitious, conceited, confident and mean. On the larger woman the words were lazy, giving, insecure, undisciplined, careless, and passive. I found synchronicity in the fact that this was exactly what I had just spoken about, and I had never seen the article before. I don't necessarily agree that we all stereotype in this way. This article was pointing me in the direction of what I needed to work on.

I had earlier discussed with my husband my thoughts about how my subconscious might be holding on to the weight because it thought that if I was thin and attractive, I might not be approachable. My clients have to trust me and feel comfortable with me. My subconscious was thinking exactly what this article was sharing, in regards to being approachable for my clients. And yet I also had felt that some people didn't choose to do business with me because of the labels that are assumed with a larger woman.

What does all this mean? Well, now I know what beliefs I need to work on, and will release any resistance that I might have. Knowing what's behind the struggle is huge in creating the needed change. I've been great with helping my clients with this process, and very grateful that I can apply all of my tools to better my own life. I hope you find some value in my thought process.

Journal Questions: What might be holding you back from being your best self? What are some negative words you've described yourself as?

I Am ALL that I say I AM...

I wrote this about my growth and myself during a writing workshop. I choose to share it with you from this perspective.

"Her radiance was contagious, when she walked into the room, everyone turned, and yet she was clueless about how she affected others. Her past was finally released and she was becoming the woman she was meant to be. For many years she believed in the "not good enoughs", so much so that she hid behind a false ego that demanded her to justify, defend and explain her every thought, action, and feeling. Her relationships seemed to be one sided, and hard, and she didn't understand why, as she tried her best to make them work, always trying to please.

The turning point, the point of release occurred, it seemed instantly, and then again, it was slow and subtle, kind of like a wakening up, a wakening up to the beauty the world had to offer. She was able to smell roses again, witness the hope of a rainbow and the gentleness of the breeze as it crossed her face. Life was opening up to her in a way that she couldn't believe.

As this awakening occurred, she was realizing that the old strenuous relationships were falling away, as if they were never there in the first place. Wonderful new things began to happen, and the more bliss she felt, the more she attracted. New relationships walked into her life, reaffirming this new journey she was on. It seemed that over time, she became that person, that person that she could not only admire, but truly love, from a deeper level than ever before. Life was good and now she knew it, felt it, shared it, in all that she is in the present moment."

Journal Questions: What are some recent "awakenings" that you've had?

Meditation, is it Really Prayer?

In recent years I have totally embraced meditation. I am sharing this as a means to encourage those silent moments. No matter what our belief or religious affiliation is, if you keep an open mind, you might find this helpful, as I did. The other night at our Prayer Chaplain meeting something wonderful was shared and I got so much out of it that I wanted to share it with others along with my thoughts and experiences with meditation.

This is from Henri Nouwen's book "Out of Solitude".

"'That evening, after sunset, they brought to him all who were sick and those who were possessed by devils. The whole town came crowding round the door, and he cured many who were suffering from diseases of one kind or another; he also cast out many devils, but he would not allow them to speak, because they knew who he was. In the morning, long before dawn, he got up and left the house, wand went off to a lonely place and prayed there. Simon and his companions set out in search of him, and when they found him they said, "Everybody is looking for you." He answered "Let us go elsewhere, to the neighboring country towns, so that I can preach there too, because that is why I came." And he went all through Galilee, preaching in their synagogues and casting out devils. (Mark 1:32-39) "In the morning long before dawn, he got up and left the house, and went off to a lonely place and prayed there." In the middle of sentences loaded with action - healing suffering people, casting out devils, responding to impatient disciples, traveling from town to town and

preaching from synagogue to synagogue - we find the quiet words: 'In the morning, long before dawn, he got up and left the house, and went off to a lonely place and prayed there.' In the center of breathless activities we hear a restful breathing. Surrounded by hours of moving we find a moment of stillness. In the heart of much involvement there are words of withdrawal. In the midst of action there is contemplation. And after much togetherness there is solitude. The more I read this nearly silent sentence locked in between the loud words of action, the more I have the sense that the secret of Jesus' ministry is hidden in that lonely place where he went to pray, early in the morning, long before dawn."

WOW! This hit me, how many times did I hurry through life? How many times did I feel the need to be doing rather than being? How much time did I take to sit in the silence, waiting to hear the answers that I so longingly wanted from outside of myself? Jesus' great example of how to handle the hustle and bustle of our everyday life is to take that quiet time for meditation. The best answers are always found in the silence. He even shared how his disciples became impatient with him for taking that time. How many times do we allow others to take those quiet moments from us?

"The words I say to you I do not speak as from myself: it is the Father, living in me, who is doing the work." (Jn14:10) "I can do nothing by myself... my aim is to do not my own will, but the will of him who sent me." (Jn5:30)

During the silence, during meditation, when we let go of the business of our days, and quiet our minds... it is then that we connect to the Divine, to our Source, to our Father God. All of life's questions and answers begin in the silence. No matter what your spiritual or religious beliefs are, this is a great reflection on how important meditation is and how the belief in the God of our understanding speaks to us in the silence. If I am too busy "doing" and not taking time "to be", there's a good chance I will miss the messages I am meant to hear and learn from.

Honor yourself by taking some time for yourself, go into the silence, it doesn't have to be before dawn, but a time and place that you won't be interrupted, where you can enjoy the stillness. I personally like to go into the water and float; I am fortunate to have a pool. I feel the sun on my face and hear the quiet sounds of nature. It is a time of bliss, where all kinds of wonderful thoughts come into my being. I also like to go into my studio and bead; the monotony and repetitiveness of the process of beading is very meditative. Choose a time and a place that works for you. Let go of all the demands of the day, and go into the silence. You deserve this wonderful blissful connection. Namaste and treat yourself to a great day!

Journal Questions: Do I take time to meditate? How do I meditate? What benefits do I get from meditating?

_____

_____

_____

Living Life With No Regrets

When we live totally present in all of our relationships, we live life with no regrets. One of the huge gifts I found in my daughter's passing, I knew that our relationship was complete. I had no regrets at all. I thought about our relationship and realized that we both were present to each other, there was nothing left back or undone.

With the technological distractions we have in our society today, living totally present, is a challenge. We are constantly reminded to look at our cell phones or social media updates. We are often preoccupied with our own problems when we are listening to others. Or we are busy thinking of our response while they are sharing. We have decided that multi-tasking is the best way to live our lives, and yet when we don't give certain things our full attention, we aren't living our best life. There are some things that don't need our undivided attention, like emptying the dishwasher or doing laundry. But when we take multitasking into our relationships we are spoiling the intimacy. Those relationships will only go so far.

It's important to practice being in the present, as our human brains are wired for survival and reaction, not necessarily peaceful responses. To practice living totally present right now, stop and focus completely on what you are doing. Consider everything that is going on with you, how you feel, what you think, and any sensitivity that you are experiencing.

Here's how to do it: whatever you're doing, right now, learn to focus completely on doing that one thing. Pay attention to every aspect of what you're doing: to your body, to the sensations, to your thoughts. If you notice bouncing thoughts, or what I refer to as "pop up personal ads", release them and come back to what you are doing and enjoy what your senses are bringing to you in the moment. It may be a smell, a sound, or what you are seeing. Continue practice doing this, and each time it will get easier and easier.

I noticed that my husband is a great conversationalist and is very detailed oriented, which I love about him. But I also know that when he wants to communicate something to me, it's in great detail, and even though I'm interested, I have a tendency to want to multi-task and only hear the "bullet points" of his conversation. Although this might work in listening to a lecture or reading a book, it definitely doesn't fare well for letting him know how much I appreciate him and his input. This is one of the areas that I have been working on to "Live Totally Present" in my life.

Journal Questions: **Where do you find yourself distracted in life, preventing you from "Living Totally Present"?**

_____

_____

_____

_____

Forgiveness

We deliberately and freely undergo a change in our emotions and attitudes about a person, place or situation; moving from victim to survivor to thrive. When we forgive, we let go of any resentments we may have in regards to the event or person. Forgiveness includes accepting that it has happened but not agreeing with or condoning it. Letting go and releasing the feelings around it, we are freed from the emotional triggers that are linked with it. There are several things that have helped me in this journey to be able to let go. First of all, trying to think and feel outside of myself, attempting to have compassion for the person that I thought inflicted the pain. A huge awakening for me was knowing that "hurt people hurt people". This allowed me to understand, not excuse, but have some compassion for what might be going on in the other person's life. My mother was abusive to me growing up, and eventually as I grew older and wiser, I thought how miserable she must be to be able to react in the ways she did. I most definitely did not want to know what it was like living in her skin. As my compassion for her grew, so did the forgiveness. You see forgiveness isn't for the other person; it is for us. When I let go and forgive, those nasty negative resentments and all the thoughts that follow go with the release. I am no longer hurt by them. I am now a thriver, not a victim. If I don't forgive, then I continue to be the victim of what happened to me, and then I am responsible from then on.

Another profound shift happened for me when I read Don Miguel Ruiz' "The Four Agreements", and I learned not to take offense. When I stopped making it about me, and didn't take offense in the first place, there were no ill feelings, no hurt, no resentments, and no reason to forgive. I learned how to stop that circle. What a relief and wonderful way to live! Sometimes I have to remind myself that it's not about me and then move on to what is my business.

One of my biggest forgiveness moments came along in October when I was at the Women's Prosperity Network's Unconference and we were encourage to write a short talk. This is what came up for me, it was huge and changed so much in my life after what the biggest tragedy I ever endured had happened.

Have you ever thought, "I've forgiven them"? I've done all the forgiveness work I need to do". Then you find out you were wrong? I was married to my children's father for 29 years and in the first ten years of the marriage I experienced physical abuse, emotional abuse, verbal abuse, financial abuse, and marital rape. After 10 years much of the abuse stopped because it became illegal in 1985. Up until then it was legal to abuse your wife, she was still considered your property. I stayed in the marriage as long as I did because I kept telling myself it wasn't that bad, and I was really trying to hold it together for the family. I also had a very low self-esteem in those years and didn't think I deserved better. Thankfully, I've done personal development work that I no longer believe that, even on the subconscious level.

After I divorced him, I spent time doing forgiveness work and thought I had released all the resentments I had. But you see I still found myself referring to him as "an asshole" and yet I don't use this language in any other conversations in my life. When my daughter, Caroline, was struck by a drunk driver, we traveled across the state to be with her. When we arrived at the hospital and saw her on life support with no brain activity, her father and I hugged for the first time in 11 years. In that instance, knowing the pain that we shared in losing our most precious daughter, I was shown that I had finally forgiven him and could no longer call him an asshole. Because I am able to see through the eyes of compassion, release resentments and forgive; or not even take offense in the first place, I can walk in the light and loving presence of the woman I was meant to be, expressing it in all things.

Journal Questions: What do you need to forgive? Starting with your self? How do you see compassion in the situation?

Meridian Tapping also known as Emotional Freedom Technique

Meridian Tapping (also known as EFT) is a self-empowering tool based on research indicating that emotional trauma contributes greatly to disease. I first learned about tapping after a car accident that left me with a back injury. I did not have any back pain until then, and didn't understand how it can affect the simple everyday actions that it does. I started tapping when I felt the pain; it helped me to sleep without pain. It also helped relieve the back pain while I was walking. I found that this simple tapping could help with a variety of different situations in my life that needed healing. You see, stress is heavily linked to pain and physical illness, as well as emotional issues. At the very least, stress escalates most illnesses; if you can reduce the stress, you can reduce the effects of the illnesses.

Clinical trials have demonstrated that Tapping (EFT) is effective in rapidly reducing the emotional consequences of memories and incidents that trigger emotional distress. After the distress is lessened or eliminated, the body frequently rebalances itself, accelerating the healing process.
Tapping uses components of Cognitive Therapy and Exposure Therapy, combining them with Acupressure, by tapping on acupuncture points.

Gary Craig was a pioneer in Meridian Tapping and founded EFT(Emotional Freedom Technique) in the 1980's while successfully working with Viet Nam Veterans suffering with Post Traumatic Stress

Disorder. He surmised "The cause of all negative emotions is a disruption in the body's energy system." He found that EFT could effectively restore the body's energy system while reducing the negative emotions.

Over 20 clinical trials published in peer-reviewed medical and psychology journals have indicated that EFT/Meridian Tapping is successful with phobias, anxiety, depression, post-traumatic stress disorder, pain, and other problems. Approximately 10 million people worldwide have used EFT or Meridian Tapping successfully with relief. I have personally used it along with others successfully. It's very empowering to know that when something comes up, you can tap away the feelings and deal with the situation in a positive way, which usually results in positive consequences. Once you learn the process, it's a simple tool that can be used anywhere and anytime.

It's important to understand that your feelings, and the energy that they have is what we are releasing. Therefore, connecting with the feelings around the circumstance while tapping is of vital importance in the releasing process. I've told many of my clients that Meridian Tapping is not necessarily polite, because so many of our feelings aren't. I explain to them the importance of explaining their feelings while tapping. In other words, tell the story of your feelings, even including tastes, smells, sounds that go with the memory of the pain, anxiety or frustration.

A good example for this is the time I was "tapping away" a craving for birthday cake. I had a huge craving and was determined to release it. While I tapped, I talked about not only the feelings I had around the craving, but also everything that went with it, even the routine way I ate the cake. Interestingly, since then I no longer crave it, nor really enjoy it anymore. I released it by connecting with the strong feelings and tapping the energy away.

I am hoping that you will utilize this powerful tool in your process of self-discovery, as the only time it doesn't work is when we don't use it. You don't even have to believe in it to work (kind of like the law of gravity, it works whether you believe it or not). However, if you do not believe in it prevents you from using it, well then of course if you don't use it, it doesn't work. At the end of each chapter, you have the opportunity to answer some questions and do some deep inner work. This is also a place to write up some things to "tap" about.

Meridian Tapping Instructions:

Rate your feelings again from one to ten, ten being the highest anxiety, fear or pain. After you do some tapping you can evaluate your feelings again, to determine how much you've released and if you need to do more tapping.

<u>Set up phrase:</u> "even though I feel _____, I deeply love, accept & forgive myself"

You will use your fingertips to tap, as the energy in your fingers is an important part of the process. Use whichever hand is more comfortable.
Tap on your hand at the karate chop point while saying **the set up phrase** above, and then continue tapping several times on the next points.

1. Tap on the top of your head, right in the middle.
2. Tap above your eyebrow towards the center of your forehead.
3. Tap at the side of your head right next to your eye.
4. Move your tapping down to the bone under your eye.
5. Begin tapping under your nose, above your mouth.
6. Tap under your mouth above your chin.
7. Tap on your collarbone.
8. Move the tapping to your side, under your armpit at chest level.
9. Tap on your hand at the karate chop point. Start over.

Tap for several rounds, until you feel relief.

Rate your feelings again from one to ten. If you've reduced the number to a 0 or 1, you are successful in creating the change, if not, tap another round or two.

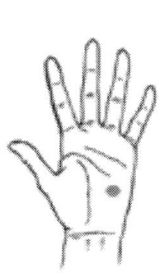

Made in the USA
Columbia, SC
17 March 2019